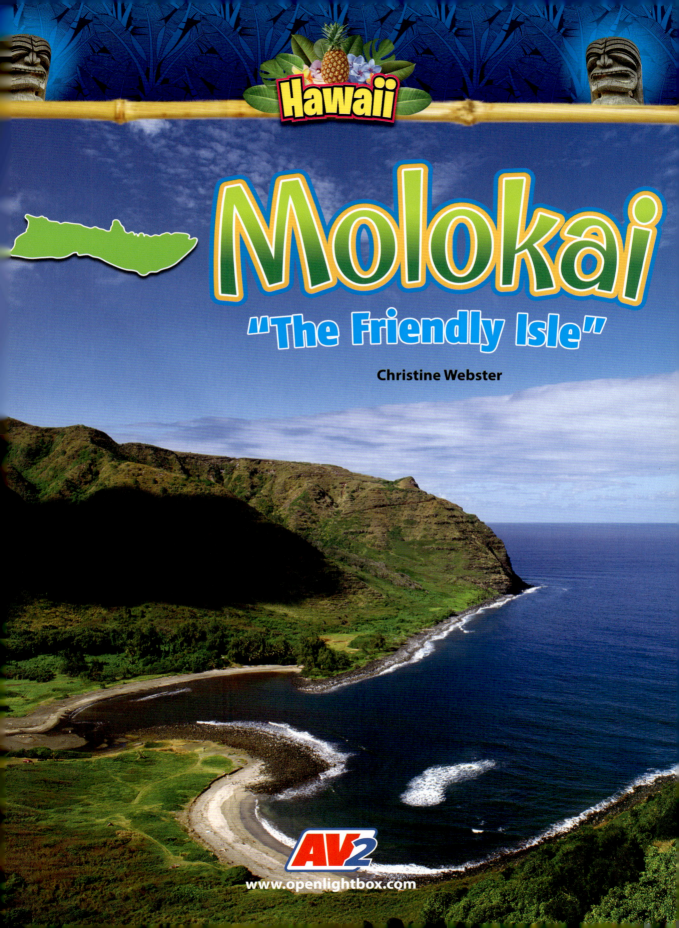

Step 1
Go to www.openlightbox.com

Step 2
Enter this unique code
OAHIF1KNX

Step 3
Explore your interactive eBook!

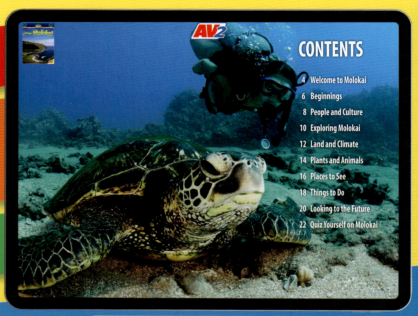

CONTENTS
4 Welcome to Molokai
6 Beginnings
8 People and Culture
10 Exploring Molokai
12 Land and Climate
14 Plants and Animals
16 Places to See
18 Things to Do
20 Looking to the Future
22 Quiz Yourself on Molokai

AV2 is optimized for use on any device

Your interactive eBook comes with...

Contents
Browse a live contents page to easily navigate through resources

Audio
Listen to sections of the book read aloud

Videos
Watch informative video clips

Weblinks
Gain additional information for research

Slideshows
View images and captions

Try This!
Complete activities and hands-on experiments

Key Words
Study vocabulary, and complete a matching word activity

Quizzes
Test your knowledge

Share
Share titles within your Learning Management System (LMS) or Library Circulation System

Citation
Create bibliographical references following APA, CMOS, and MLA styles

This title is part of our AV2 digital subscription

1-Year Grades K–5 Subscription
ISBN 978-1-7911-3320-7

Access hundreds of AV2 titles with our digital subscription.
Sign up for a FREE trial at www.openlightbox.com/trial

The digital components of this book are guaranteed to stay active for at least five years from the date of publication.

Hawaii

Molokai
"The Friendly Isle"

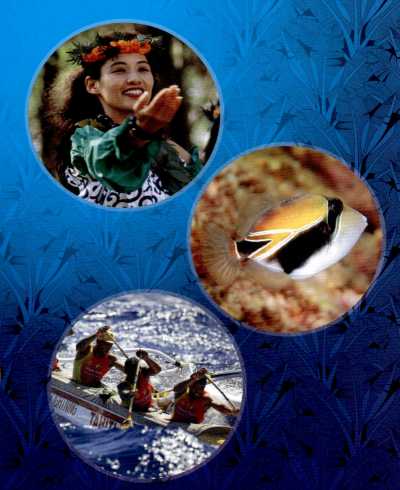

CONTENTS

- 2   Interactive eBook Code
- 4   Welcome to Molokai
- 6   Beginnings
- 8   People and Culture
- 10 Exploring Molokai
- 12 Land and Climate
- 14 Plants and Animals
- 16 Places to See
- 18 Things to Do
- 20 Looking to the Future
- 22 Quiz Yourself on Molokai
- 23 Key Words/Index

MOLOKAI—The Friendly Isle

WELCOME TO Molokai

Molokai receives **fewer than 1,000** visitors per day.

Molokai is **38 miles** (61 kilometers) long and **10 miles** (16 km) wide.

In 2024, the town of Kaunakakai had **3,574 people** living in it.

HAWAII

Aloha! Welcome to Molokai! Molokai is one of the islands that make up the U.S. state of Hawaii. It is part of the Hawaiian Islands, an **archipelago** in the Pacific Ocean. The archipelago has more than 130 different islands. Molokai is the fifth-largest Hawaiian Island.

Molokai's nickname is "The Friendly Isle." It is known for its friendly, down-to-earth people. Molokai is also called the "most Hawaiian" island. A large number of the people who live on Molokai are of Hawaiian **descent**, ensuring that Hawaiian culture continues to thrive there.

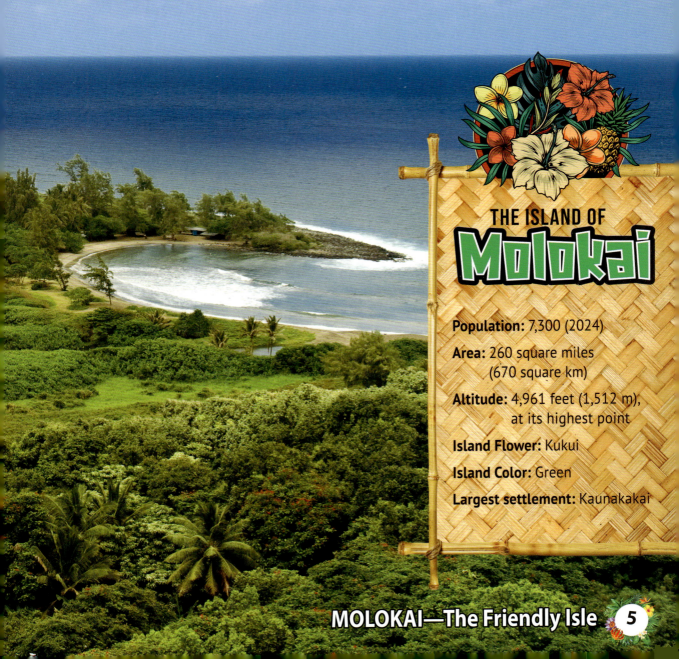

THE ISLAND OF Molokai

Population: 7,300 (2024)

Area: 260 square miles (670 square km)

Altitude: 4,961 feet (1,512 m), at its highest point

Island Flower: Kukui

Island Color: Green

Largest settlement: Kaunakakai

MOLOKAI—The Friendly Isle

Beginnings

About 2 million years ago, two volcanoes rose from the Pacific Ocean. This event created the island of Molokai. Today, the volcano known as Kamakou makes up eastern Molokai, while Maunaloa rises up in the west.

Approximately 1 million years ago, the northern third of Molokai broke off and fell into the ocean. Steep cliffs mark where the break took place.

Polynesians were the first people to settle on Molokai. They arrived about 1,400 years ago. In 1786, a British explorer named Captain George Dixon became the first European to set foot on the island. Other Europeans soon followed. In the 1830s, a **contagious** disease called leprosy began spreading throughout the Hawaiian Islands. People with the disease were sent to live in a leprosy **colony** on Molokai. Most lived out the rest of their lives at the site.

In 1897, approximately 70,000 acres (28,300 hectares) of Molokai's land were purchased for a ranch. Cattle and other livestock were raised there. Cowboys roamed the land. For more than 100 years, Molokai Ranch was the island's biggest employer.

Molokai Ranch shut down operations in 2008. Both the land and buildings, including the lodge, are now waiting for a new owner.

Speaking Hawaiian

The word *molokai* means "Gathering of Ocean Waters." It is pronounced "moh-loh-kai."

HAWAII

Molokai Timeline

650 AD
Polynesians begin to settle on Molokai.

1786
Captain George Dixon lands on the shores of Molokai.

1795
King Kamehameha I assumes control of the islands of Maui, Lanai, Oahu, and Molokai on his way to ruling the entire Hawaiian archipelago.

1865
The Hawaiian government approves the creation of a leprosy colony on Molokai.

1897
Molokai Ranch is established.

2024
A brushfire comes close to Molokai's airport before being contained. Residents are evacuated, and roads are closed.

MOLOKAI—The Friendly Isle

People and Culture

Approximately 50 percent of Molokai's residents are **native** Hawaiians, making them the island's largest cultural group. **Traditional** Hawaiian values and lifestyles are a big part of island life on Molokai. The people are known for their *aloha* spirit. They are welcoming and ready to help others. Molokai retains a rural feel, with most islanders working on **plantations** and ranches. While some work in tourism, it is not a large industry on the island.

Molokai is said to be the birthplace of hula, a form of dance that honors the **ancestors** of today's Hawaiians. Hula movements are graceful and fluid. Dancers typically perform them to the sounds of stringed instruments and drums. Sometimes, the dances are accompanied by chants. These chants are used to document legends or history.

Each year, the people of Molokai celebrate hula with a festival called *Ka Hula Piko*, or "Center of the Hula Dance."

Speaking Hawaiian

In Hawaiian, *e komo mai* means "welcome." It is pronounced "eh koh-moh my."

Island events are the best way to experience the culture of Molokai. Many celebrate the way of life on Molokai and show what is important to the people who live there. The island holds its Ka Molokai Makahiki Festival every January. This honors a past tradition, when Hawaiians would come together in peace to celebrate the end of the harvest. Traditional sporting events, food, crafts, and hula are big parts of this festival.

The Molokai Hoe canoe race between Molokai and Oahu is held every year to pay tribute to the inter-island canoeing of Hawaii's past.

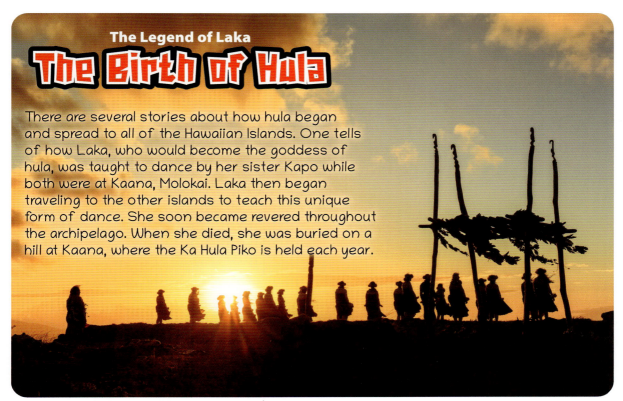

The Legend of Laka
The Birth of Hula

There are several stories about how hula began and spread to all of the Hawaiian Islands. One tells of how Laka, who would become the goddess of hula, was taught to dance by her sister Kapo while both were at Kaana, Molokai. Laka then began traveling to the other islands to teach this unique form of dance. She soon became revered throughout the archipelago. When she died, she was buried on a hill at Kaana, where the Ka Hula Piko is held each year.

MOLOKAI—The Friendly Isle

Exploring Molokai

Molokai is known for its unspoiled beauty. With no large cities and limited commercial development, the focus is on the natural aspects of the land. Pristine beaches, sparkling waterfalls, dramatic cliffs, and lush **rainforests** dominate the landscape.

Kaunakakai

Located on Molokai's south shore, Kaunakakai is the main place on the island to shop, dine out, and stay overnight. Known as a cowboy town, it has maintained its rural charm. Most of the buildings were built in the late 1800s and early 1900s.

Kamakou Preserve

The Kamakou Preserve is a rainforest found on the slopes of Kamakou. Covering an area of 2,774 acres (1,123 ha), it is home to various plants and animals, many of which are unique to Molokai. The large amount of rain that falls on the preserve makes it an important water source for the island.

Kalaupapa Peninsula

This **peninsula**, on Molokai's north shore, covers an area of about 5 square miles (13 sq. km). A wall of 2,000-foot (600-m) tall cliffs separates it from much of the island. This was why it was chosen to be the site of the island's leprosy colony.

Moaula Falls

One of the highlights of the Halawa Valley is Moaula Falls. This waterfall has several tiers, but only two are visible from the ground. Together, these two have a drop of about 250 feet (76 m).

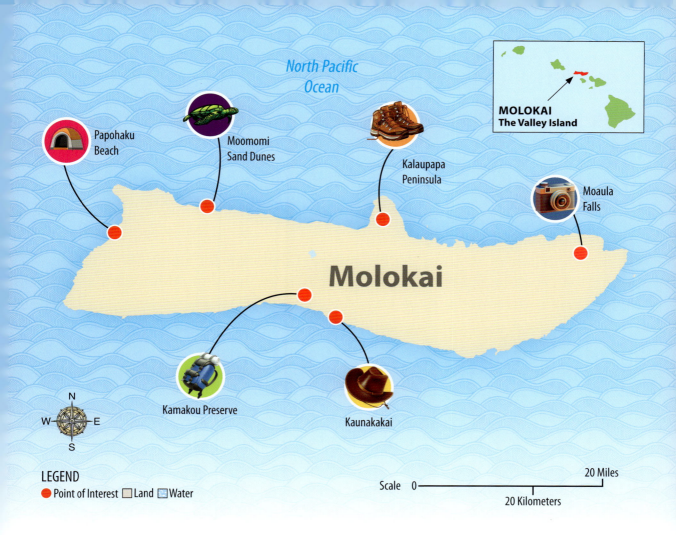

Moomomi Sand Dunes
One of the few sand dune **ecosystems** left in Hawaii, the Moomomi Sand Dunes extend about 1 mile (1.6 km) in length and are hundreds of feet (meters) wide. The dunes are home to about 22 native plant species. They are also an important nesting site for green sea turtles.

Papohaku Beach
This is one of Hawaii's longest white-sand beaches. It is known as the "Three Mile Beach" because its soft sand stretches for 3 miles (4.8 km). People often come to the beach to camp or picnic and take in the view of the neighboring island of Oahu.

MOLOKAI—The Friendly Isle

Land and Climate

The volcanoes that created Molokai form two distinct parts of the island, East and West Molokai. They are separated by the Hoolehua Plain, a flat area covering about 28,000 acres (11,300 ha) of land. West Molokai is considered the drier of the island's parts, lending itself well to the kiawe forests that are found there. East Molokai, being more moist, is known for its rainforests and waterfalls.

On the south side of Molokai is a fringing **reef** that runs for about 28 miles (45 km). A type of coral reef, it grows directly from the island. Molokai's fringing reef is the longest in the United States.

No point in Molokai is more than 5 miles (8 km) from the ocean.

Speaking Hawaiian

Ua is a Hawaiian word for "rain." It is pronounced "oo-ah."

12 HAWAII

Like other Hawaiian Islands, Molokai has a **tropical climate**. This means that it has warm temperatures all year. The island's average annual temperature is 75 degrees Fahrenheit (24 degrees Celsius).

Precipitation levels can vary in different parts of the island. While the west averages about 20 inches (500 millimeters) of rain per year, the east typically receives about 35 inches (900 mm). The rainforests in the east can receive more than 300 inches (7,600 mm) of rain each year.

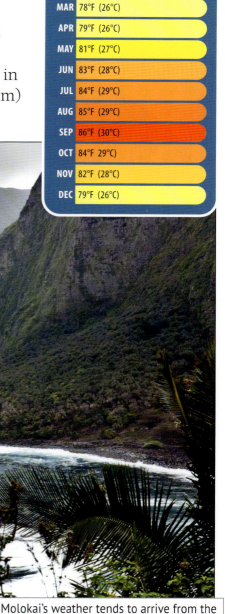

Average High Temperatures

Month	°F	°C
JAN	77°F	25°C
FEB	77°F	25°C
MAR	78°F	26°C
APR	79°F	26°C
MAY	81°F	27°C
JUN	83°F	28°C
JUL	84°F	29°C
AUG	85°F	29°C
SEP	86°F	30°C
OCT	84°F	29°C
NOV	82°F	28°C
DEC	79°F	26°C

Molokai's weather tends to arrive from the northeast. Heavy clouds sometimes stall on the island's northern cliffs, causing rain to fall there.

MOLOKAI—The Friendly Isle

Plants and Animals

Molokai is home to many species of plants and animals. Some of these are common throughout the Hawaiian Islands. Others can only be found on Molokai.

White Molokai Hibiscus

This hibiscus is **endemic** to Molokai's rainforests. The bushes grow to about 10 feet (3 m) in height. Their white blooms can be more than 4 inches (10 centimeters) long. The flowers give off a faint fragrance, which is rare for plants in the hibiscus family.

Apapane

The apapane belongs to a group of birds known as honeycreepers. These birds rely mainly on nectar for food, but may also feed on insects from time to time. The apapane is common on most of the main Hawaiian Islands, where it is mainly found in forested areas.

HAWAII

Reef Triggerfish

Also known as the humuhumunukunukuapuaa, the reef triggerfish is Hawaii's official state fish. It can be found swimming in coral reefs throughout the Hawaiian archipelago, where it feeds on algae, snails, and sea urchins. Reef triggerfish can reach a length of about 8 inches (20 cm). They are known for their distinct markings.

Hawaiian Centipede

The Hawaiian centipede can grow to be more than 14 inches (36 cm) in length. It typically lives under rocks and leaves. This centipede is **venomous**, but rarely lethal to humans. It uses its venom to kill prey such as earthworms, spiders, and small insects.

Molokai Jackbean

The Molokai jackbean is a climbing plant with reddish-purple blooms. This member of the pea family is endemic to Molokai and is found mainly on the eastern part of the island. Here, it grows in dry areas on steep cliffs.

Dwarf Naupaka

Dwarf naupaka grows only on Maui and two of Molokai's small islets, where it is found in rocky areas along the coastline. It grows close to the ground and rarely exceeds 6 inches (15 cm) in height. Its cream-colored flowers produce purple berries.

MOLOKAI—The Friendly Isle

Places to See

People often come to Molokai to experience its natural beauty. Palaau State Park offers guests views that include pastures, forests, and sea cliffs. The Kakahaia National Wildlife Refuge is home to several species of **endangered** animals. Visitors can look out over the rainforest at the Molokai Forest Reserve.

Molokai has historical and cultural attractions as well. Kalaupapa National Historic Park was created to preserve the memories of Molokai's leprosy colony. The park features the original housing provided to the colony's residents, as well as churches and other community buildings. Visitors must apply for a permit to enter the park. This is because some of the former leprosy patients still make their homes there.

Pathways in Palaau State Park allow visitors to walk through dense ironwood forests.

Saint Philomena Church is one of the key structures in Kalaupapa National Historic Park. It was both built and expanded upon by the colony's early residents.

HAWAII

The Molokai Museum and Cultural Center, near Kaunakakai, pays tribute to Molokai's early settlers through videos, photos, and personal accounts. The island's agricultural past is highlighted with a restored sugar mill. Other exhibits expand on the island's development over the years.

Molokai's agricultural heritage can also be experienced with a trip to Purdy's Nut Farm. The farm's original macadamia orchard was planted more than 100 years ago. Since then, the farm has gone on to add candlenuts and coconuts to its product line as well. Tours offer visitors the chance to learn about the farming practices used to grow these plants.

Visitors to the Molokai Museum and Cultural Center can view the equipment settlers used to make sugar. This includes the cane crusher, which ran with the help of mules.

In addition to learning about nut farming, visitors to Purdy's Nut Farm can sample the nuts grown there.

Molokai has only **one hotel**, but there are condominium resorts with rooms to rent.

About **350,000 people** visit Molokai each year.

The average visitor to Molokai spends about **$200 per day**.

MOLOKAI—The Friendly Isle

Things to Do

Molokai is a hub for outdoor activities. Many of them focus on the ocean surrounding the island. Molokai's waters are very calm, making them perfect for snorkeling and scuba diving. The fringing reefs are a popular spot for an underwater experience. Here, divers are likely to see Hawaiian monk seals, sea turtles, and schools of tropical fish.

Scuba divers are most likely to encounter green sea turtles while diving in the waters around Molokai.

Riding on the water is another way to spend time in Molokai. Local **outfitters** offer kayak and stand-up paddle tours along the island's coast. In the winter months, guests can take whale-watching tours to see the humpback whales that come to Molokai's waters to breed.

Molokai's outfitters offer kayaking tours for all skill levels.

Speaking Hawaiian

The Hawaiian word for **humpback whale** is *kohola*. It is pronounced "ko-ho-LAH."

18   HAWAII

A cultural hike is a unique way to explore Molokai's interior. Led by islanders themselves, these hikes take visitors past some of Molokai's best-known landmarks. The history and legends behind these sites are relayed to foster a deeper understanding of the island and its people.

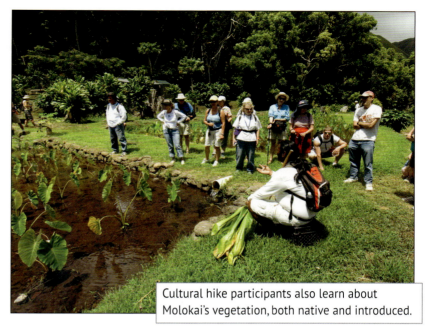

Cultural hike participants also learn about Molokai's vegetation, both native and introduced.

Biking is another way to explore Molokai. The island has several established bike trails, with a range of difficulty levels. The Molokai bike path is an easy ride that connects the towns of Kaunakakai and Maunaloa. The East Molokai Loop is more challenging but offers spectacular coastal views.

Some riders take their bikes along Molokai's scenic sea cliffs.

MOLOKAI—The Friendly Isle

Looking to the Future

Molokai's residents value their way of life. They appreciate the small-town atmosphere their island has and want Molokai to stay as it is. While they are welcoming to visitors, they do not actively pursue the tourist trade. As tourism is a key industry throughout Hawaii, this approach has meant that Molokai's economy is not as strong as other parts of the state.

The islanders are working to find ways to help their economy while keeping their ideals. While some locals have formed traditional tour companies, others are now adopting a different approach to welcoming guests. Instead of having people drop in for a day to see a few sights, they encourage visits by people who want to immerse themselves in island culture and interact with the locals more. Programs are in place that allow guests to engage in volunteer work or help out on local farms, for instance. To the people of Molokai, this makes the visits more mutually rewarding.

Some local companies offer day tours of Molokai, allowing guests to get an overview of the island in a short amount of time.

HAWAII

Ferries between Molokai and Maui had been running for 30 years when the service ended in 2016.

As one of the least-visited Hawaiian Islands, Molokai can also fall victim to a reduction in services. For years, a **ferry** operated between the islands of Molokai, Maui, and Lanai. Locals used it to reach jobs and access health services on other islands. When the ferry stopped operating in 2016, Molokai's access to inter-island transportation was limited to one airline offering only a few flights per day.

The local government has been reviewing the situation to see how it can be fixed. One possible solution is the creation of a government-run ferry service between the three islands. Another suggestion has been the extension of the runway at Molokai's airport to allow larger aircraft. However, the extent to which this will increase tourist traffic to the island must also be considered.

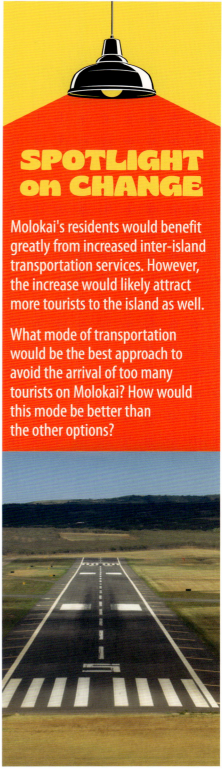

SPOTLIGHT on CHANGE

Molokai's residents would benefit greatly from increased inter-island transportation services. However, the increase would likely attract more tourists to the island as well.

What mode of transportation would be the best approach to avoid the arrival of too many tourists on Molokai? How would this mode be better than the other options?

MOLOKAI—The Friendly Isle

QUIZ YOURSELF ON Molokai

1. What is Molokai's largest settlement?
2. What is Molokai's island color?
3. Who was the first European to set foot on Molokai?
4. What percentage of Molokai's population is native Hawaiian?
5. What is Molokai's nickname?
6. What is the name of the flat area that separates East and West Molokai?
7. What is the state fish of Hawaii?
8. Which park was created to preserve the memories of Molokai's leprosy colony?

ANSWERS: 1. Kaunakakai **2.** Green **3.** Captain George Dixon **4.** Approximately 50 percent **5.** "The Friendly Isle" **6.** Hoolehua Plain **7.** Reef triggerfish **8.** Kalaupapa National Historic Park

HAWAII

Key Words

ancestors: people who were in someone's family in past times

archipelago: a group of islands

climate: the average weather conditions of a particular place or region over a period of years

colony: an area where people with illness or special needs are set apart from others and live together

contagious: capable of being spread from one person to another through direct or indirect contact

descent: the background of a person in terms of family or nationality

ecosystems: communities of organisms and their physical environments interacting together

endangered: threatened with no longer existing on Earth

endemic: native and restricted to a certain place

ferry: a boat used to carry passengers, vehicles, or goods

native: occurring naturally in a particular area

outfitters: businesses that sell clothing, equipment, and services for outdoor activities

peninsula: a piece of land that is almost entirely surrounded by water

plantations: agricultural estates worked by laborers

Polynesians: Indigenous people who come from the islands of Polynesia

rainforests: dense forests that receive heavy annual rainfall and are made up of tall evergreen trees whose tops form a continuous layer

reef: a chain of coral, rock, or other hard material near the surface of water

traditional: based on information, beliefs, or customs handed down from one generation to another

tropical: relating to the hottest parts of the world

venomous: able to inflict a poisoned bite, sting, or wound

animals 10, 11, 14, 15, 16, 18, 22
biking 19
cultural hike 19
Dixon, Captain George 6, 7, 22
Halawa Valley 10
Hoolehua Plain 12, 22
hula 8, 9
Ka Hula Piko 8, 9
Kakahaia National Wildlife Refuge 16
Kalaupapa National Historical Park 16, 22
Kalaupapa Peninsula 10, 11
Kamakou Preserve 10, 11
Kamehameha I, King 7
Ka Molokai Makahiki Festival 9
Kaunakakai 4, 5, 10, 11, 17, 19, 22
Lanai 7, 21
leprosy 6, 7, 10, 16, 22
Maui 7, 15, 21
Moaula Falls 10, 11
Molokai Forest Reserve 16
Molokai Museum and Cultural Center 17
Molokai Ranch 6, 7
Moomomi Sand Dunes 11
Oahu 7, 9, 11
Palaau State Park 16
Papohaku Beach 11
plants 10, 11, 12, 14, 15, 16, 17, 19
Purdy's Nut Farm 17
scuba diving 18
snorkeling 18
tourism 4, 8, 16, 17, 18, 19, 20, 21
whale watching 18

MOLOKAI—The Friendly Isle 23

Get the best of both worlds.
AV2 bridges the gap between print and digital.

The expandable resources toolbar enables quick access to content including **videos**, **audio**, **activities**, **weblinks**, **slideshows**, **quizzes**, and **key words**.

Animated videos make static images come alive.

Resource icons on each page help readers to further **explore key concepts**.

Published by Lightbox Learning Inc.
276 5th Avenue
Suite 704 #917
New York, NY 10001
Website: www.openlightbox.com

Copyright ©2026 Lightbox Learning Inc.
All rights reserved. No part of this publication may be reproduced, stored in a retrieval system, or transmitted in any form or by any means, electronic, mechanical, photocopying, recording, or otherwise, without the prior written permission of the publisher.

Library of Congress Cataloging-in-Publication Data

Names: Webster, Christine, author.
Title: Molokai "the friendly isle" / Christine Webster.
Description: New York, NY : Lightbox Learning Inc., [2026] | Series: Hawaii | Includes index. | Audience: Grades 2-3
Identifiers: LCCN 2024047336 (print) | LCCN 2024047337 (ebook) | ISBN 9798874506711 (lib. bdg.) | ISBN 9798874506728 (paperback) |
    ISBN 9798874507541 (ebook other) | ISBN 9798874506735 (ebook other)
Subjects: LCSH: Molokai (Hawaii)--Description and travel--Juvenile literature. | Molokai (Hawaii)--Social life and customs--Juvenile literature.
Classification: LCC DU628.M7 W434 2026 (print) | LCC DU628.M7 (ebook) |
    DDC 919.69/24--dc23/eng/20241211
LC record available at https://lccn.loc.gov/2024047336
LC ebook record available at https://lccn.loc.gov/2024047337

Printed in Guangzhou, China
1 2 3 4 5 6 7 8 9 0 28 27 26 25 24

122024
101124

Project Coordinator: Heather Kissock
Designer: Terry Paulhus

Photo Credits
Every reasonable effort has been made to trace ownership and to obtain permission to reprint copyright material. The publisher would be pleased to have any errors or omissions brought to its attention so that they may be corrected in subsequent printings. The publisher acknowledges Getty Images, Alamy, Shutterstock, and Wikimedia as its primary image suppliers for this title.

View new titles and product videos at **www.openlightbox.com**